Neighborhood Safari

Bees

by Dalton Rains

www.focusreaders.com

Copyright © 2025 by Focus Readers®, Mendota Heights, MN 55120. All rights reserved. No part of this book may be reproduced or utilized in any form or by any means without written permission from the publisher.

Focus Readers is distributed by North Star Editions: sales@northstareditions.com | 888-417-0195

Produced for Focus Readers by Red Line Editorial.

Photographs ©: Shutterstock Images, cover, 1, 4, 6, 8, 10, 12, 14, 17, 18, 21

Library of Congress Cataloging-in-Publication Data
Names: Rains, Dalton, author.
Title: Bees / by Dalton Rains.
Description: Mendota Heights, MN : Focus Readers, [2025] | Series: Neighborhood safari | Includes bibliographical references and index. | Audience: Grades K-1
Identifiers: LCCN 2023054185 (print) | LCCN 2023054186 (ebook) | ISBN 9798889981725 (hardcover) | ISBN 9798889982289 (paperback) | ISBN 9798889983392 (ebook pdf) | ISBN 9798889982845 (hosted ebook)
Subjects: LCSH: Bees--Juvenile literature | Bees--Anatomy--Juvenile literature | Bees--Behavior--Juvenile literature | Bees--Life cycles--Juvenile literature
Classification: LCC QL565.2 .R35 2025 (print) | LCC QL565.2 (ebook) | DDC 595.79/9--dc23/eng/20231220
LC record available at https://lccn.loc.gov/2023054185
LC ebook record available at https://lccn.loc.gov/202305418

Printed in the United States of America
Mankato, MN
082024

About the Author

Dalton Rains is a writer and editor from Minnesota.

Table of Contents

CHAPTER 1
Back to the Hive 5

CHAPTER 2
Body Parts 9

CHAPTER 3
Spreading Pollen 13

We Need Bees 16

CHAPTER 4
A Bee's Life 19

Focus on Bees • 22
Glossary • 23
To Learn More • 24
Index • 24

Chapter 1

Back to the Hive

A bee lands on a flower. The bee sips the flower's **nectar**. It also gathers **pollen**. Then the bee brings the pollen back to its hive.

Some kinds of bees live in hives. A hive is made up of many small cells. Each cell has six sides. Some of the cells have **larvae** inside. Other cells store food.

Fun Fact

Not all bees live in hives. Most bees live alone. They build small nests for themselves.

Chapter 2

Body Parts

Bees are insects. A bee has six legs. It has two pairs of wings. A bee also has two **antennae** on its head. Some bees have stingers. Others do not.

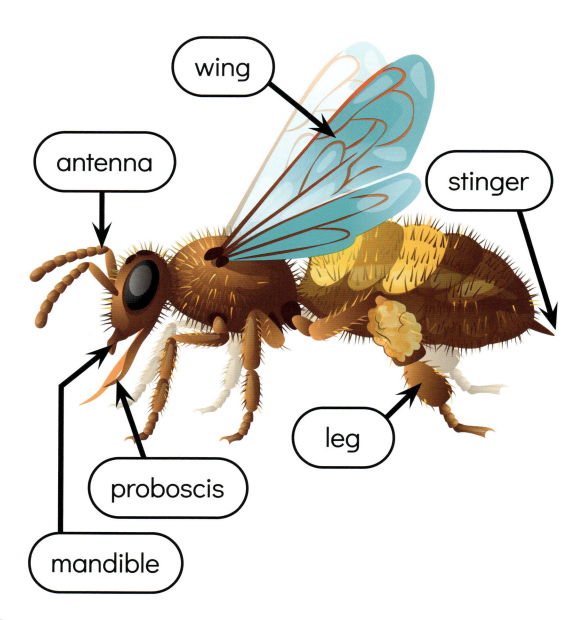

A bee has mouth parts called mandibles. Mandibles help the bee bite and cut. Every bee also has a proboscis. This part is shaped like a straw. The bee uses its proboscis to suck up liquid.

Fun Fact

Some kinds of bees are smooth. Other kinds are fuzzy.

Chapter 3

Spreading Pollen

Bees fly from flower to flower. They eat pollen and nectar. Pollen gets on their bodies. Later, it rubs off on other flowers. That helps plants **reproduce**.

Some bees use nectar to make honey. They store the honey inside their hives. They can feed it to larvae. Or they eat it during winter.

Fun Fact

Sometimes people make hives for bees to live in. Then they take some of the bees' honey.

That's Amazing!

We Need Bees

Many plants depend on bees. Apples and berries would not grow without bees. But bees are in trouble. Some types of farming hurt them. **Pesticides** can kill them. Farming without pesticides helps bees stay healthy. Planting more flowers can help bees, too.

Chapter 4

A Bee's Life

Bees start life inside cells. First, larvae hatch from eggs. Larvae eat and grow. Next, they become **pupae**. After a few weeks, they are adults. Then, they leave their cells.

Different kinds of bees have different jobs. The queen bee lays eggs. Female worker bees gather food. They also build new cells. Male bees are called drones. They **mate** with the queen.

Fun Fact: Queen bees can lay more than one thousand eggs every day.

Life Cycle

- The queen bee lays eggs in open cells.
- After a few days, the eggs hatch into larvae.
- Worker bees feed the larvae.
- After two weeks, the fully grown larvae turn into pupae.
- Pupae turn into adults and leave their cells.

FOCUS ON
Bees

Write your answers on a separate piece of paper.

1. Write a few sentences describing how bees get food.
2. Would you want bees to live near your home? Why or why not?
3. What kind of bee lays eggs?
   - A. worker
   - B. drone
   - C. queen
4. What might happen to plants like apple trees if bees were not around?
   - A. The plants might not reproduce.
   - B. Many more plants might grow.
   - C. The plants might change color.

Answer key on page 24.

Glossary

antennae
Long, thin body parts on an insect's head. The parts are used for sensing.

larvae
The young, active forms of insects.

mate
To come together to make a baby.

nectar
A sweet liquid made by plants.

pesticides
Sprays that kill unwanted plants or animals.

pollen
A powder from male parts of plants. It spreads to female parts of plants to make seeds.

pupae
Insects that are growing from larvae into adults.

reproduce
To make more of a living thing.

To Learn More

BOOKS

Murray, Julie. *Bees*. Minneapolis: Abdo Publishing, 2020.

Sabelko, Rebecca. *Bee*. Minneapolis: Bellwether Media, 2021.

NOTE TO EDUCATORS

Visit **www.focusreaders.com** to find lesson plans, activities, links, and other resources related to this title.

Index

F
flower, 5, 13, 16

H
hive, 5, 7, 15

I
insects, 9

M
mandible, 10–11

N
nectar, 5, 13, 15

P
proboscis, 10–11

Answer Key: **1.** Answers will vary; **2.** Answers will vary; **3.** C; **4.** A